Movers, Shakers and Record Breakers

20 Stories from British History

Geraldine McCaughrean was born in North London and has a degree in Education. She has been writing full time for many years and has won the Whitbread Award, the Guardian Children's Fiction Award, the Carnegie Medal and, most recently, the Blue Peter Book Award.

Movers, Shakers and Record Breakers is the last in a series of five books which will include all 100 stories from *Britannia: 100 Great Stories from British History*.

Also by Geraldine McCaughrean

Britannia: 100 Great Stories from British History
Britannia on Stage
God's People
God's Kingdom
Stories from Shakespeare

100 World Myths and Legends
incorporating The Golden Hoard,
The Silver Treasure, The Bronze Cauldron,
The Crystal Pool

Knights, Kings and Conquerors
Rebels and Royals
Daredevils and Desperadoes
Ghosts, Rogues and Highwaymen

Movers, Shakers and Record Breakers

20 Stories from British History

Geraldine McCaughrean

Illustrated by Richard Brassey

TED SMART

This edition first published in Great Britain in 2002
by Dolphin paperbacks
a division of the Orion Publishing Group Ltd
Orion House
5 Upper St Martin's Lane
London   WC2H 9EA

The stories in this volume were originally published
as part of *Britannia: 100 Great Stories from British History*,
first published by Orion Children's Books in 1999.

This edition produced for
The Book People Ltd
Hall Wood Avenue,
Haydock,
St Helens WA11 9UL

A catalogue record for this book is
available from the British Library

Printed in Great Britain by
Clays Ltd, St Ives plc

ISBN   1 85881 895 8

Contents

Introduction

In this last volume of stories, there are no more knights and kings, no more giants or dragons. The real heroes are ordinary people – some cleverer than most, some braver, some more desperate, some more driven.

These stories are largely true: in a scientific world, history itself has become a science. Time itself is up for grabs, whether in charting the evolution of man or breaking the four-minute mile. The outside world encroaches on our little island – a world full of menace, pollution, ideas and possibilities. Sense as you read how the setting subtly expands: world war, global pollution, a hungry planet.

In the nineteenth and twentieth centuries Britannia stood up and walked out into the world.

The *Rocket* Speeds to Victory
1829

"Now lads, I venture to tell you that I think you will live to see the day when railways will supersede almost all other methods of conveyance in this country, when mail coaches will go by railway and railroads will become the great highways for the King and all his subjects." In the heady excitement of the opening, George Stephenson's words swept his employees up on a tide of enthusiasm. They cheered and stamped their heavy boots. But could it really be true? Could railways really be the transport of the future? Here, at Stockton, they were busy assembling a 90-ton train the like of which had never been seen before: six freight wagons, a covered coach for VIPs, twenty-one coal wagons kitted out to carry 450 passengers, and six more full of coal! And *Locomotion* was supposed to pull it – an engine barely taller than a man, Stephenson's brainchild. In front rode a horseman holding a green flag – almost as if they were going into battle.

But as the train gathered speed, Stephenson had to shout for the flag-man to get out of the way. Other riders galloping alongside for the sport of racing the train were left far behind, as *Locomotion* accelerated to the fabulous speed of 15 miles an hour (24 kph)! There was a hero's welcome waiting in Darlington –

and 150 more passengers and a brass band wanting to join the return journey to Stockton.

The Stockton–Darlington line, though, was just a freight line – a means of shifting large quantities of coal very cheaply along a shuttle line. When it came to building the first passenger line, from Liverpool to Manchester, the investors employed George Stephenson as chief engineer, laying the tracks, but announced a competition to find the best locomotive for the route. The deadline was 6 October 1829, the prize £500.

This time George worked with his son Robert to develop his entry for the competition. They incorporated a tubular boiler, which allowed large quantities of water to be heated up at any one time. There were two other locomotives entered: Braithwaite and Ericsson's *Novelty*, and the *Sans Pareil* built by Hackworth. Between 6 and 14 October, there was a gala atmosphere at Rainhill, Liverpool, with huge crowds attending every day, bands playing and a great grandstand seating such dignitaries as the Duke of Wellington, then Prime Minister.

The referees looked over the *Sans Pareil* and declared it did not comply with the rules . . . but she would be allowed to compete anyway. The course was a stretch of track rather more than two kilometres in length, which had to be completed, there-and-back, ten times over. On the eighth trip the pump broke and the *Sans Pareil* puttered to a halt.

The crowd had taken a fancy to the *Novelty*: it was small and spry, with only the vestige of a chimney, and a jolly red flag flying. But with an alarming bang, the boiler blew after just two trips. "And they say these things will take the place of horses?" people snorted to one another.

Up and down, up and down, up and down went the *Rocket*. Tireless as a donkey giving rides on a beach, the *Rocket* lumbered to and fro. Pulling a load of 17 tons, she travelled the 30 miles stipulated – then she travelled them again to please the crowds. At one point she touched 30 mph (18 kph) – faster than any stagecoach could go. The crowd was a roaring sea of cheers, thousands of day trippers witnessing this dawn of a new age. The Duke of Wellington stood up in the bandstand and waved his hat as Stephenson's *Rocket* trundled by yet again, steam flaring from the crown-shaped tip of its sturdy flue.

One year later, a similar locomotive was coupled up to thirty-three carriages, all packed with notables: the Duke of Wellington, Sir Robert Peel, the Rt Hon William Huskisson MP for Liverpool ... and steamed out of Liverpool to the music of an on-board band. Despite the flying smuts which blackened their faces and clothes, despite the noise, and the juddering of the hard seats, the passengers were cock-a-hoop. They were in at the beginning of something momentous. Here was history in the making!

At Parkside, the train wheezed to a halt to take on water. Some of the gentlemen passengers, including Mr Huskisson, got off to stretch their legs. They strolled down the track ... ignorant of the fact that another string of carriages was moving down the adjacent track. As they saw the danger, the knot of men scattered, all jumping clear of the tracks, except for Mr Huskisson, who tried to re-board the train.

He got the carriage door open, but it swung back on him and barged him off his feet – knocked him on to the rails, in fact, where one of the great slicing, steel wheels rolled over him.

Suddenly there was no more music, no more singing, no more cheering. As the litter bearers carried the man away and the locomotive gathered speed, its steam cast a pall over thirty-three silent carriages. Women dabbing cinders from their eyes, dabbed away tears as well. It was no longer a day of triumphant celebration. William Huskisson had died of his injuries. The festivities planned in Manchester were cancelled. George put his arm around his son's shoulders. "There's no undoing what's done," he said. "No going back."

ROBERT
STEPHENSON

George Stephenson was the uneducated son of a miner on Tyneside where he started work at the mines. He graduated to pithead winch-operator, earned extra money mending boots and clocks in the evening, learned to read at evening class, then married and had a son. Little Robert would come home from school and teach his father everything he had learned that day, while George would share with Robert his latest flashes of inspiration.

The Resurrection Men
1829

"Another one for the graverobbers, eh, William?" said Burke. "Disgraceful trade. Fancy a man engaging in a Godless business like that, William," replied Hare with a snigger. "Sacrilege, I call it."

Many of the graves in the cemetery had recently been surrounded with great iron railings – as though the dead had been penned into their plots. But then, understandably, mourners did not want grave robbers digging up their nearest and dearest within hours of them being laid to rest. And there was a thriving market for bodies dug up on dark nights among the lowering yew trees. The medical profession needed its cadavers and would pay good money for one, without asking where it came from. The police were cracking down, patrolling cemeteries, making arrests, but even so, today's grave would have a grille of iron around it before nightfall.

The crunch, crunch of the constable's boots on the pavement behind them held no fear for Hare and Burke. Their conciences were clear. As far as they were concerned, the crack-down on grave-robbing could only serve to boost business; they were not in that line of work.

"Our meat is *fresher*, eh William?" whispered Hare, and lifted his hat to the constable.

Burke and Hare went home to their wives, and their wives agreed: there were easier ways to lay hands on supplies than wrestling iron bars in the graveyard and dodging watchful policemen. They all went out to an inn for supper, and struck up a friendship there with a young man.

"Won't you come home for a nightcap?" asked Mrs Hare. "William and I do so welcome company…"

Burke set down a sack in the ill-lit basement yard, and money changed hands. Their customer was bursting to tell them of a comical story he had just read in his newspaper. "Did you hear tell of the old woman who sneezed?" he snickered. "I read they opened the coffin – and up she sat and sneezed! Ha! ha! ha!"

"There's no fear you'll be troubled in that way," muttered Hare. "This one died of natural causes three days back." There was a brief glimmer of light as the sack was taken in at a basement door, then renewed darkness.

Next day, as the student doctors crowded about the scrubbed dissecting table of Edinburgh University, the corpse upon it was the finest yet. It showed no sign of decay. It had surely never lain underground, in the damp Edinburgh clay. In fact the young man lying dead on the table looked very much as he had looked in life, apart from a certain blueness in the face.

"Good God! I know him!" exclaimed one of the students, turning deathly white.

"Didn't you know he was dead? Didn't anyone tell you he died?" his colleagues asked, each wondering how he would feel if the body in front of him proved not to be a nameless stranger.

"And how would they? I was *drinking* with him last night!" spluttered the student.

"I fear our friends have overstepped the mark this time," remarked Dr Knox.

But he continued his lecture. For it was hardly *his* fault if Burke and Hare had graduated from grave-robbing to cold-blooded murder. And there was no point in wasting such an excellent cadaver.

Ever since medicine became a clinical science, there has been a need for cadavers or dead bodies. Students of medicine need to dissect bodies to understand the nature and workings of human anatomy. In nineteenth-century Edinburgh (as elsewhere) they were kept supplied by body-snatchers who stole newly-buried corpses from graveyards. In Edinburgh, Doddingston Village churchyard was frequently pillaged by these so-called "Resurrection Men".

Fortifying the graves, and a police crackdown in the 1820s helped to stamp out the practice. But some body-snatchers simply resorted to a worse way of acquiring bodies. William Hare and William Burke may never even have bothered to rob graves. They were arrested in 1829 for murdering fifteen people for the sake of their cadavers. Their wives had helped them lure victims to their deaths. Hare offered to co-operate in return for supplying evidence which sent Burke to the gallows; in fact he was probably the worse villain of the two.

Victoria's Room
1837

"I cried much," wrote Alexandrina Victoria in her diary that night. She was eleven years old, and she had just been told the secret her mother had been keeping from her: one day she would be queen.

Why did she cry? Perhaps she was afraid. Perhaps she could see ahead of her a life of unrelenting hard work, never free to do as she liked. Maybe she thought that the loneliness of her childhood would now go on for ever.

At least now she could make sense of all the studying her mother made her do, all the huffy unkindness of her English relations who looked upon her as a little German interloper, all the loneliness.

Once a week, a child was invited to play – a child chosen by her mother. Not the same child every week, so that they could become firm friends. Never anyone silly or mischievous who might make her laugh – just a succession of miscellaneous strangers, once a week. "I may call you Jane, but you must not call me Victoria," she would tell them, not knowing why, only knowing that life was governed by her mother's rules. She had her dolls – her host of elegant china-headed dolls. But somehow they were not the same as having a true friend.

For all she was a princess, no one showered her with

toys or treats or sweets. No, it was bread and milk out of a little silver bowl for Victoria. She was not allowed to read stories: after all, what *use* were stories except for frivolous entertainment?

Lonely but never alone, Victoria could not even escape to the solitude of her own bedroom. Every night she had to bed down in the great hollow emptiness of her mother's bedroom, and every time she woke, it was to the sound of her mother's soft breathing. Sixteen, seventeen, eighteen, and still she was sharing a bedroom! How she longed for a room of her own.

Victoria woke one morning sensing that something momentous had happened. Her mother was whispering

to her in German: to get up, to put on her wrapper; there was an important visitor to see her. Fuddled with sleep, her heart jumpy with odd foreboding, Alexandrina Victoria fumbled her feet into her satin slippers and made herself presentable.

As soon as she saw the Archbishop of Canterbury, po-faced, holding himself as he did at state occasions, she knew that someone had died. It was her Uncle William, he told her. The King of England was dead.

With a rustling flurry, like a theatre curtain falling, the ladies in the room sank down. For a moment Victoria thought they had fainted with shock, but no. They were curtseying to their new monarch — to her — to eighteen-year-old Queen Victoria.

A million thoughts and images tumbled through her head in those first few moments: the hot, distant countries she had never seen and over which she now held absolute sway. Those dark, frightful valleys she had visited with her mother, where coal dust had turned all the people and houses and grass coal-black. All those huge cathedrals and little parish churches where every day from now on prayers would be offered up for "Victoria our Queen". The Houses of Parliament which smelled of leather and passed the laws to which she must now set her signature. The marriage which would now be arranged for her — how she hoped it could be to cousin Albert! She thought of the pageant of kings and queens which had already filed past into history, of the soldiers in red who would die for her in foreign wars. All these thoughts and more fell like an avalanche on Victoria, on this tiny, slender girl in her night clothes.

But her first command, as Queen of England, was for a room to be prepared: a room of her own.

"I will try to fulfil my duty towards my country and to do what is fit and right," she wrote that night. And when she closed her diary, the room around her listened in respectful silence. Though a thousand choices were closed to her, she felt a new sense of freedom. It was up to her now, how she lived the lonely life of a queen.

Her china-headed dolls sat quietly round, watching her, outnumbered now by millions of other loyal subjects.

After moving to Buckingham Palace, Victoria arranged for her mother's suite of apartments to be a long way from her own. By 1840, she was no longer lonely: she had married her cousin Albert – a suitable candidate found for her by her family, but a love-match as far as Victoria was concerned. They were to have nine children.

The English monarchy was in a bad state when Victoria came to the throne. A string of kings, mad, bad or just plain despised had brought royalty into disrepute. She changed all that. She ruled for longer than any other monarch in the history of England. Albert fired her with enthusiasm and energy for all kinds of projects, including the Great Exhibition of 1851. She was a devoted mother, had a will of steel and ruled at a time when the economy was, in any case, thriving. In 1876, she became Empress of India. The British people, the British Empire, adored their little Queen, and when Albert died and she retired into perpetual mourning, they resented her absence from public life. She died aged eighty-one and gave her name to an entire era.

Fire Down Below

1838

Dr Dionysius Lardner said it couldn't be done. No steamship could carry enough fuel, he said, to voyage more than 2,000 miles, and America was 3,000 miles away; it was totally impractical to talk of sailing steamships between England and New York.

The shipping companies prayed he was wrong. To win the race across the Atlantic was everything. The rewards would be huge to whichever steamship company could first prove Dionysius Lardner mistaken!

Whichever ship was first across the Atlantic was certain to make headline news. Already the *Sirius* was preparing to set sail from Cork in Ireland – the furthermost westerly point. But a rival ship was out to

beat her – and to beat her in style, sailing not from Ireland but from England, a day farther east.

On Saturday, 31 March, the SS *Great Western*, dream-child of Isambard Kingdom Brunel, set sail from Blackwall Docks in London. Down the Thames, round the south coast and she would be in Bristol, bound for New York. There were passengers in plenty ready to sail on her: after all, her designer was an acknowledged genius. Brunel had built bridges and viaducts, railways and tunnels. He had spanned gorges and linked cities . . . and now he had turned his attentions to the Atlantic.

But at the mouth of the Thames, disaster struck. The brand-new felt cladding the brand-new boilers caught fire, filling the engine room with dense, choking smoke. Captain Claxton ran the *Great Western* ashore on the mudflats and everyone tackled the fire.

Claxton himself went down into the noxious fumes and the heat. Overhead, flames were licking the underside of the decking. The boiler was singing with heat. The great pillars of steel, like the columns of a

Greek temple, were ringing with a discordant music all their own. Claxton called for the fire-hose to be turned on and directed it at the fire which hissed steam, in addition to the smoke and fumes. Soon he was ankle-deep in water, and the fire reduced to sullen red embers glimmering in the corners of the boiler room like the eyes of a hundred rats.

All of a sudden, a weight like a sack of grain fell on him from above, knocking all the wind out of him. He cursed choicely and picked himself up. What had hit him? Who was dropping things on to him from the open hatchway? None too gently, he felt for the thing with his foot: it was soft and sodden. A man! And, lying face-down in dirty water, he was either dead already or about to drown! Instantly Claxton snatched hold of him. Then he cursed again. "Hoi! Up there! Fetch ropes! Hurry! It's Brunel! He's fallen!"

In climbing down to help Claxton, Brunel had rested his foot on a burned rung which gave way. If Claxton had not been standing underneath, he would have crashed on to metal from a dizzying height.

Claxton tied a rope under his friend's armpits, and somehow they manhandled Brunel up through the funnelling smoke and steam towards the blue square of the forehatch. Even laid out on deck, with a sail for a bed, he remained unable to speak. But until the fire was under control there was no time to care for him any more tenderly.

They set him ashore at Canvey Island, and sailed on without him. They were in Bristol within forty-eight hours. It astounded the crowds who had heard tell of the fire and quite thought the *Great Western* a burned-out hulk in the Thames estuary. Here she was, with nothing to show for the fire but a few scorchmarks.

They would not sail on her, though. Only seven passengers were ready to put their faith in the *Great Western*; the rest had been scared off by the fire. For those seven it was a memorable voyage. One wrote in his journal that New York harbour was crowded with welcoming boats, "Flags were flying, guns were firing, and cheering rose from the shore, the boats and all around loudly and gloriously . . . It was a moment of triumph."

Not that they had won the race: *Sirius* had arrived just hours before, despite departing earlier and farther west. But *her* coal had been all used up, and her crew had had to burn everything combustible on board – including passengers' luggage – just to make harbour. The *Great Western*, on the other hand, had used only three-quarters of her fuel. Dr Lardner had been proved wrong: steamships *could* link England and America.

Sixty-eight passengers made the return voyage to England, and for twenty years the SS *Great Western* plied the oceans of the world, a handsome tribute to her designer. When she was broken up in 1857, Isambard Kingdom Brunel was there to bid her farewell.

I.K. Brunel began his career working for his engineer father. He went on to become chief engineer of the Great Western Railway, designing lines, trains, sheds and stations, then set his sights on grander, interlinked networks of travel. After the *Great Western* came the *Great Britain*, at that time the biggest ship in the world, the first with an iron-hull, the first to be driven by a screw-propeller rather than paddle-wheels. Next came the monumental *Great Eastern*, four times larger, capable of carrying a year's exports to India in one trip.

In no other age could Brunel have achieved what he did. The Victorian passion for technology put him to work and, in return, he added hugely to Victorian prosperity. Bridges, railways, buildings, ships, tunnels, viaducts still exist today as monuments to his genius.

Saving Grace
1838

It was four in the morning when Grace pulled on her clothes and climbed the stairs to the light. It was her turn to check the lighthouse lamp then sit up, so that her father could get to bed. All around her the storm raged: torrential rain and the everlasting thunder of the sea rolling against England's north-east coast, breaking against the Longstone Rock, throwing its spray as high as her bedroom just below the lamp. The noise of it drowned out even the click of the lighthouse engine as she sat in her room watching for first light when she must douse the light. Her window was cloudy with condensation from her wet stockings and petticoat. She and Father had got soaked through the previous afternoon, lashing down the coble-boat.

It was not until she went back up the steep steps to put out the light that she looked across towards Brownsman Island to glimpse her old home and saw not the abandoned buildings of Brownsman Island but the huge, dark looming prow of a ship.

"Father! Father! Father! A wreck! A wreck, Father!" she shouted, running backwards down the spiral stairs. "A ship is wrecked on Big Harcar!"

"Now God help us, and your brother not here!"

From five till seven they stood there in the lamp room, William Darling holding a telescope, Grace a pair of field glasses. The stormclouds kept the scene almost as dark as night, and all they could make out was that the vessel was a steam paddle-ship – the *Forfarshire*, perhaps. And if it were the *Forfarshire*, William knew there were probably sixty people on board. It was not until the eye of the storm passed over the reef that a shaft of light, like God's own sword-blade, lit Big Harcar and showed the huddle of people clinging to the rock itself.

"Can it be done, Father?" asked Grace.

"Maybe, if Brooks were here."

It was true, that if Grace's brother, Brooks, had been at home that night, instead of on the mainland, he would have gone with his father in the coble – gone to try to lift those people off before the sea did. "Then I must take Brooks's part!" said Grace.

Her mother was dead set against it. She had heard the bang of the maroons – the signal which summoned out the lifeboat – and she knew the coble needed three strong men to row it in rough weather.

But William Darling knew the lifeboat would never arrive in time. The sea's huge swell heaved up like a great grey tongue to lap at the survivors. He must mount a rescue mission or stand and watch those people washed away, one by one.

Instead of a tender goodbye, Grace got nothing but reproach from her mother, who said she would hold Grace to blame if William drowned. Grabbing up a shawl, a blanket and a bonnet, and slipping off her flannel petticoat to save it getting soaked, Grace helped her father unlash the rowing boat. Spray covered her like thick, white sheets. The oars rattled like bones in

their rowlocks. But Grace rowed. Sometimes the water tried to wrench the oar out of her hand, at others she found herself scooping at empty air, but she went on rowing. She rowed alongside her father, her shoulder against his, as though through a tunnel of sea. She rowed until her hands were full of blisters. All she could think of were those other cold, white hands clinging and clawing, slipping and losing their grip on the treacherous rocks. Big Harcar was no more than a perch for puffins, a basking place for seals; its rocks disappeared with every breaking wave.

They could not row there direct, but had to let the wind drive the little boat south, into the lee of the reef and then row in from there. And *if* there was someone there, among the survivors on the rock – some strong, uninjured man not yet perished with cold or mad with fright – they might just be able to make the rescue and get back to the lighthouse. If not, there was no chance. Grace and her father would join the casualties lost in the sinking of the steamer.

Back in the lighthouse, Mrs Darling watched for a sight of them. Despite a lifelong horror of heights, she dragged herself up one flight of stairs after another, hoping each one would raise her high enough to see over the towering waves. But the little coble had utterly disappeared, as if the sea had swallowed it whole. Fainting with horror, it was not until she came round that she glimpsed it – pitching like a shuttlecock over the mountainous swell.

There were nine on the rocks, including one woman, clasping her two dead children, not realizing the cold had stolen them from her. And there *was* a seaman still calm, still strong enough to pull on an oar. For a few horrific minutes, William Darling leapt across to the rock, and Grace was left trying to hold the boat steady, all alone, with oars set so far apart that her arms were at full stretch just to grip them.

Five people were taken off. The other four had to wait for the coble to make a return trip. Two of the men agreed to go with William on that second voyage. So while Mrs Darling and Grace wrapped the survivors in blankets and plied them with black tea, the lighthouse keeper went out again into the storm, which was working itself into a frenzy. Grace and her mother hardly expected to see him again. But finally, finally, he and the other six staggered in, dumb with weariness, numb with cold, their faces caked into masks by the sea's salt.

Like the pillar of stillness at the centre of a tornado, the Longstone Lighthouse cocooned those twelve people until the sea slackened, the clouds cleared and the rain ceased to fall. While they waited, William Darling wrote up his report on the wreck, mentioning only in passing that nine lives had been "saved by the Darlings". Little did he know what a storm of praise, congratulation, publicity and admiration would break over their heads when the rescue was reported. When people read in their papers of the lighthouse keeper and his brave daughter, Grace's adventure had only just begun.

Grace and her father were both awarded gold medals from the Royal Humane Society and silver medals for bravery by the "Shipwreck Institution", a forerunner of today's Royal National Lifeboat Institution. (In fact Grace has been cited as an inspiration behind the founding of the RNLI.) She also received £100 reward, and Queen Victoria wrote to her in person, praising her bravery. But as she battled her way through the storm of publicity and was acclaimed a national heroine, some local Northumbrians grew bitter and insulting, suggesting she had done it for the money. She was the butt of hate mail and malicious lies. The money, in any case, would have bought her little in the way of happiness: four years after the wreck of the *Forfarshire*, Grace Darling died in her father's arms, of tuberculosis.

Rebecca and Her Daughters

1840s

"And they blessed Rebekah and said unto her, Let thy seed possess the gate of those which hate them." That was the verse which began it. That was where the Bible fell open, those were the words which sprang off the page. Just when every Welsh heart was brooding bitterly about having to pay tolls to the Government – just to be allowed to pass along a road! – there was the Good Book speaking out on the matter. And the Welsh have always taken their Bible seriously.

Dafyd, the Turnpike, keeper of the toll-gate on the London road, woke to the sound of horns and whistles and gunfire, and tumbled out of bed. Along the road came a crowd of people led by five or six women – at least they were *dressed* like women. They wore bonnets and dresses and aprons, though to judge by the size of their boots, they were six feet tall and shaved once a week. The people in the procession behind them were locals – poor hill-farmers, dyers and tradesmen. Dafyd knew it, though it was hard to make out particular faces in the dark.

"Now I don't want no trouble," said Dafyd, trying to sound commanding (though that is difficult for a man in his nightshirt). "Why don't you all go off home now?"

The biggest of the "women" simply turned to the

crowd and said, in a ringing Welsh bass, "My children, this gate has no business here, has it?"

The crowd roared, "No, Mother, it has not!"

"Then what is to be done with it, children?"

"Mother, it must be levelled to the ground!"

Then the axes came out. Rebecca and her Daughters were destroying yet another toll-gate, hacking the bars from their cross-trees, the hinges from their posts.

Dafyd ran a few steps forwards. After all, he was paid to man the gate; he ought to defend it. But the Daughters restrained him with huge, calloused hands. "We mean you no harm, man. Best just pack up your things."

Knowing that already half the toll-gates in Carmarthen were down, Dafyd hurried indoors and began to carry his few possessions – bed and chair, breadbin and toolbag – out of doors. Then the toll-booth too was destroyed – set alight with Dafyd's own lantern.

The horns and whistles blew, the guns sent Dafyd's cat haring into the wood, then "Rebecca and her Daughters" were gone. The local people disbanded silently and the darkness swallowed them up.

Within the hour, a detachment of special constables came trotting along the road to where Dafyd sat in his fireside chair on the grass verge of the road. "You're too late, as usual," he said. "Far too late."

In Carmarthen that June, thousands of protesters carrying placards, scythes and pitchforks marched into the town and began pulling down the workhouse. Beds were tumbled out of windows; pots and pans rained on to the cobbles. To poor, working people, the workhouse represented everything wrong with society: a prison for the poor, where the only crime of the inmates was to be penniless. That's why they tore it down. For long enough the rich landowners and businessmen had grown fat on the toil and tolls of the poor. Now that was all about to change.

The magistrates went out to remonstrate with the mob, reading them the Riot Act: "You are hereby charged to disperse peaceably . . ."

The mob washed over them like the sea over sandcastles.

Then the dragoons arrived from Cardiff – a sixty-mile gallop from barracks. Two of their horses dropped dead as they entered the city, but for the first time the rioters were obliged to break off from their vandalism and run.

The dragoons used the flat of their swords, not the

sharp edges. After all, they were Welshmen themselves, from poor Welsh homes, and knew injustice when they saw it. They scattered the mob and took a hundred prisoners, but they did it gently, almost sympathetically.

Before long, Rebecca and her Daughters regrouped stronger and more determined. There was no *one* Rebecca, you see. No *one* ringleader. The men in bonnets and aprons began to meet in secret and to list their demands, instructing the magistrates, the landowners, the Church to dismantle their toll-gates or to expect a bullet through the window or a fire in their stables.

Righteous anger had given way to thuggery and terrorism. One night, an old woman on the Glamorgan-Carmarthen border was shot dead in cold blood, just for manning a toll-gate. The law had become so weak that the inquest jury declared she had died from a "suffusion of blood...cause unknown". The coroner did not even dare condemn the crime of murder.

But when the toll-gate in Gower Street, in the heart of London, was filed off its hinges overnight the Government felt the Welsh problem had come too near to home. It stirred itself like a sleeping dog. The movement was destroyed, hacked apart as ruthlessly as any toll-gate or turnpike booth. It imprisoned the ringleaders or sent them to a life of hard labour in Australia.

But while, with one hand, the authorities meted out prison sentences and transportations, with the other hand it wrote legislation for the abolition of toll-gates from the nation's public roads. So the sound of those horns and whistles and pistols, the swish of petticoats and the tramp of worn boots *had* been heard, even from the other end of the long London Road.

The early years of Queen Victoria's reign were marked by huge social unrest. Poverty and hardship caused by an economic depression gave rise, in 1838, to the Chartist Movement, which agitated for every man to have the vote and for reform of Parliament. The Charter petition was signed by so many that when rolled along the lanes to London, it was the size of a cartwheel. Parliament ignored it. A "Chartist" rebellion at Newport, Wales, in 1839 was put down with great ferocity. This is the setting into which Rebecca and her Daughters were born. The many anonymous Rebeccas would have been Chartists to a man.

Father of Nobody's Children
1869

At six o'clock the children said a prayer then clattered towards the door. Some were more eager than others: it was cold outside. One boy dawdled at his desk, wiping his slate, and dropping his chalk. "Run off home, boy," said the teacher.

"Please, sir. Let me stop."

"Nonsense. It's time to go. Your mother will wonder what is keeping you."

"I ain't got no mother." The lad scuffed a bare foot on the plank floor.

"Where do you live, then?"

"Don't live nowhere."

The teacher sighed. After ten hours teaching he was weary and wanting his supper. He did not know the boy by sight – every day new pupils found their way to the charity school; he hoped this was not going to be some hard-luck story. Barnardo knew home life was hard – downright miserable – for most of the children attending his ragged school. But he had never set much store by melodramatic tales of children living rough on the streets, parentless and homeless. That was just romantic exaggeration. Surely. "Where did you sleep last night?" he asked.

"Down Whitechapel, sir, along o' the Haymarket, in one of them carts as is filled with 'ay. Then I met a chap

33

as telled me to come up 'ere to school and you'd maybe let me lie near the fire all night. I won't do no harm, sir, if you let me stop."

A coldness blew through Barnardo which had nothing to do with the bitter weather. "Is it possible?" he asked himself. Then he asked Jim Jarvis: "Are there other boys who do that – sleep where they can – out in the open?"

"Oh yes, sir, lots. Heaps on em! More'n I could count!"

Barnardo took Jim Jarvis home and gave him hot coffee. He was a perky lad, witty and cheerful – except for his eyes where some drowning-depth of sorrow contradicted the saucy grin. Over supper Jim told his

life story. From the age of five he had been on his own, fending for himself, an orphan. He got work with a man called "Swearing Dick" on the barges who beat him regularly, and threatened to set his dog on Jim if he tried to run away. A job on a market stall was no better. It was the police he feared most, because they would either kick him or arrest him and send him to the workhouse.

At about midnight, Barnardo set off with Jim Jarvis to see the boy's "lay", as he called it. Jim led the way to Petticoat Lane, to an old-clothes market, where he scrambled up on to the iron roof of a shed. Reaching down a stick, he helped Barnardo up too. Alongside was a hayloft and, though it was padlocked shut, some of the hay had trickled out through the slats. Eleven boys had grubbed together these wisps and were lying stretched out on them now, on the tilt of the roof, feet in the guttering. They lay close-huddled for warmth, like hamsters in a nest. No blanket over them, no clothes capable of keeping out the cold. Their sleeping faces were white and thin as skulls.

"The foxes have their holes, the birds their nests, but the Son of Man has nowhere to lay his head."

Thomas Barnardo had thought God was calling him to go to China, to be a missionary. For years he had cherished the idea – only really filling time in London, until his posting came through. Now, all of a sudden, he realized: God had not been whispering "China" in his ear. God had been bellowing in his face: "Help these children. Save these children. They have no one but you. They are nobody's children but yours and Mine!"

Barnardo could not bear it. To wake the boys would

have been like fetching the dead from their graves. They would clamour at him for food, turn those hollow, reproachful eyes on him. The horror of their loveless, hopeless lives gripped him as he climbed down, legs trembling. Jim Jarvis watched him, bird-like, head cocked on one side, but the doctor could say nothing, do nothing but walk away, striding out faster and faster, until he was almost running.

Thomas J. Barnardo founded a home for homeless boys and soon afterwards another for girls. He was tireless in his efforts, not only to help the children but to enlighten the comfortable middle classes who genuinely did not know what was happening in the streets of their Victorian cities. He tackled all the social evils, turning drinking halls into evangelical tea-halls, turning drunkards and criminals into evangelists. He taught and preached, raised money, wrote articles and addressed public meetings. He told the story of Jim Jarvis many times, embroidering it considerably over the years but always to good effect.

A complex man, Barnardo gave himself the title "doctor" though he never qualified as one. He was criticized for "staging" the photographs he sold to raise funds: before-and-after photographs of his forlorn street children. Hugely slandered, hugely admired, he drove himself repeatedly into a state of nervous collapse. But his homes multiplied, his message got through. Barnardo Homes became an institution of British life for which thousands and thousands of children, right up to the present day, have had cause to be thankful.

The Last Train Ride

1879

Everyone was in a hurry to get home – Scotsmen returning to Scotland for the holidays, families who had been south for Christmas, workers anxious to get back to the warmth of a fireside and a good supper . . . Though Christmas was over, the New Year was still to come.

It was a filthy night, but the lights of Dundee burned all the brighter for that. And crossing over the Tay

would be part of the fun. The new bridge was still a wonder to those contemplating a trip over it – a stone and metal monument to progress and prosperity.

By seven in the evening, the wind was howling, hurling itself against the signal boxes as if it would swallow them whole; unfurling dense, silver banners of rain across the starless sky. With each new gust, the carriages juddered and the luggage jumped about in the luggage van. Children with their noses pressed to the steamy windows would recoil against their mothers, then be drawn back to cloud the windows even more with their excited breathing. The noisy rhythm of the wheels on the track – "nearly-there-nearly-there nearly-there" – was all but drowned out by the storm.

Then, all of a sudden, the countryside of lashing trees and huddled buildings gave way to rainy darkness: the train was crossing the Firth of Tay (though the river far below was not even visible through the rain). The locomotive gave a baleful whistle which the wind tore in shreds.

Two signalmen stood discussing the safety of their signal box – whether it might blow down, whether the storm would blow itself out by morning or racket on into Hogmanay. The London–Dundee train went by them wrapped in its cloak of sooty steam, slowing down for the bridge. Out over the Tay it thundered, a snake of lights, a wisp of white steam. Then a plume of sparks rose up – golden rain amid the silver. There was a tremendous flash.

Too far off for sound to carry. But as the signalmen watched, the snake of lighted carriages disappeared abruptly from sight.

Passengers on board, tumbled together by sudden braking, felt nothing now – nothing but an absence of sound. Oddly, for a second or two, the rain outside the windows rained upwards, because they were falling so fast. No time for anything more than a joining of hands, then the Tay was boiling over the wreckage and the storm was hooting.

Running down to the foreshore, the two signalmen shouted out at every tight-closed front door they passed: "*The bridge! The bridge! The train!*" But when they reached the mudflats (where the waves were breaking big as the open sea) there was nothing to do but stare into blackness. With a triumphant flourish, the storm uncovered the moon, briefly casting a ghastly, ghostly pallor over the river. The whole centre section of the Tay Bridge was gone, like a smile with its teeth smashed away. The train must have driven out on to thin air, then plunged into the deep, icy water of the Tay.

Next day, divers were needed to find the sunken train, rolled and scoured by the river's current. Of the seventy-nine people aboard, not one lived to see in the New Year of 1880.

The bridge, 3¼ kilometres (nearly 2 miles) long, had only been open for nineteen months when on 28 December 1879 half a dozen of its central spans collapsed into the river. 1880 claimed the eightieth victim of the disaster. Architect Sir Thomas Bouch (who had designed the bridge with insufficient strength to withstand even low winds) died, vilified and reproached for his incompetence. A second, unfinished bridge of his had been found to be as dangerous as the first.

Fortunately or unfortunately, the disaster was immortalized by the so-called poet William McGonagall in a work of such awfulness that it is performed today as a comic turn. He followed it up with an ode to the beautiful *new* Tay Railway Bridge, which was completed in 1890.

Dr Crippen on the Waves
1910

Not for the first time, Captain Henry Kendall wiped the glass of the bridge-house and peered at the couple on the deck below: Mr Robinson and son. In his many years at sea, Kendall had developed an eye for oddities among his passengers, and there was something distinctly odd about Mr Robinson and son.

Why, for instance, did they stay so muffled up in this fine July weather? And why, when they thought no one was looking, were they *holding hands*?

Before setting sail, he had read newspaper descriptions of a couple wanted for murder. Old newspapers were probably still lying around the ship detailing the sensational crime. As far as he remembered, a dentist's wife had been done to death, her body cut up and hidden under the floorboards. Her husband, mysteriously gone missing with a lady friend called Ethel, was number one suspect. Captain Kendall's thoughts returned time and time again to the description of the man called Crippen.

And yet this ship had set sail from Antwerp in Belgium, not from Britain. Could Crippen have escaped to Belgium before the body of his wife was found? Could this be him now, trying to reach Canada and a new life with his accomplice? Was "Master

Robinson" the reason Hawley Crippen had murdered his lawful wedded wife?

Captain Kendall left the bridge and strolled down to the sundeck. Casually he struck up conversation with Mr Robinson and son, though the two seemed in no mood to talk. Robinson's lids were slightly closed and there were pad marks on the bridge of his nose, though he had not worn glasses since boarding.

Dr Crippen had worn glasses.

Robinson's top lip was paler than the rest of his face. He had recently shaved off a moustache.

And Dr Crippen had worn a moustache.

The son wore a trilby hat several sizes too big, and an awkward, hesitant smile. His hands were very small and pale, and his coat too broad for his shoulders.

Kendall was certain. But what to do about it? The SS *Montrose* was outside British waters now, and, when it docked in Canada, Crippen would be on foreign soil. He might get clean away.

At least he might have got clean away, had he taken passage on a less modern ship.

Kendall hurried along to his brand-new radio room and told his brand-new radio operator, "Here's a job for you. Radio London and tell them we have Dr Hawley Crippen and his lady friend Ethel aboard."

When Chief Inspector Walter Dew received the telegraph from Captain Kendall, he left at once for the docks. He took passage aboard the SS *Laurentic*, a faster ship than the *Montrose*. In a matter of days, he could overhaul Kendall's ship and be in Canada ahead of Crippen. But the arrest must be made aboard the British ship, and that meant boarding her before she docked. Nothing must be left to chance.

"Mr Robinson!" said Captain Kendall, and the little man gave a visible start. His top lip was no longer white, thanks to the sea air, but his expression was still nervy and anxious. "Soon be there now," said Kendall, bluff and jovial. "I have just taken aboard the local pilot to see us safely into the mouth of the St Lawrence River. I wondered, would you and your son care to meet him?"

Mr Robinson and his son exchanged glances. He smiled weakly. "Delighted, I'm sure." The shores of Canada were within sight. A new life was so close that Hawley and Ethel could almost smell it. Where was the harm in accepting the captain's invitation? They could not very well refuse.

As they entered the captain's cabin, a man stood up. He was not their idea of a shipping pilot: a tall man in a bowler hat and overcoat.

"Hawley Harvey Crippen . . . Ethel Le Neve – I arrest

you for the murder of Belle Crippen on or before 9 July 1910."

The little man trembled violently from head to foot; the woman beside him clutched the sleeve of his coat. "Thank God it's over," said Crippen. "The suspense has been too great. I couldn't stand it any longer." And meek as a lamb, he allowed Chief Inspector Dew to handcuff him and lead him away.

DR. CRIPPEN

US-born Dr Hawley Crippen was the first criminal to be captured through the invention of ship-to-shore radio. He disappeared from his home in Camden Town on 9 July, shortly before police discovered his wife's dismembered body under the floorboards. The mild-mannered dentist had escaped from England with his lover, Ethel Le Neve, and reached Belgium undetected. But on 20 July, they boarded the SS *Montrose* bound for Quebec. The arrest took place on 31 July. He was promptly returned to London and charged at Bow Street court one month later. He was hanged on 23 November the same year.

The First and Last Voyage of the *Titanic*

1912

Ben Guggenheim slipped his arms into the silk-lined sleeves of his evening jacket and turned to his cabin mirror to fasten his tie. "What say we take a turn around the deck and listen to the band?" he said to his secretary.

Outside, on deck, it was a beautiful, frosty, starlit night – only a chilly breath of a breeze and a calm, smooth sea. The ship was ablaze with lights. The band played a lively little dance number from its huge repertoire. An altogether perfect evening . . . were it not for the screaming.

All round, people were praying and running, sobbing and swearing, hugging or struggling to climb up high. Steerage passengers were still streaming up from the lower decks, and the ship groaned in agony as its back prepared to break.

"Unsinkable" they had said in the advertisements: "the ship that cannot sink". The newspapers had made much of her size and safety, her luxury and collision-proof double hull. Pride of the White Star Line, the *Titanic* was the last word in elegance and technology. People had flocked to buy tickets for her first voyage – the rich and glamorous, quite at home beneath the chandeliers of her immense ballroom, poor Irish emigrants who could only afford the smallest, cheapest cabins on their trip to a new life in America. The ship was a little world in miniature: rich on top, poor on the bottom, but all heading in the same direction. And she was so *big* – the length of London's Shaftesbury Avenue, and just as brightly lit!

The iceberg, by contrast, moved like a dirty brown slab, hidden for the most part underwater. It had broken away from the polar pack ice to float aimlessly south across the shipping lanes. And it too was titanic.

The look-out Fred Fleet saw it at the last moment and shouted a warning, clanged the alarm bell three times. The ship seemed only to graze against the great ice hulk, then sail by, a rattle of ice skittering across the decks. "That was a close shave," said Fleet to himself.

But there was a ninety-metre gash below the waterline, a gash which had pierced both layers of the double hull and buckled the whole structure. Icy water was already pouring in. The "unsinkable" *Titanic* had two hours to live.

The bow and wheel-house were already underwater, but the stern was still afloat and reasonably level. One of the huge funnels disintegrated and toppled into the water amid the swimmers and rafts and life-boats.

There had not been enough lifeboats – not enough for even half the people aboard. A strange oversight. Perhaps on an unsinkable ship, lifeboats had not seemed important. Some boats had capsized on launching. As a result, the lifeboats, floating now within the glow of the ship's lights, were crammed with precious cargoes of silks, satins, furs and diamonds. Women and children first. That is the rule at sea.

Of course some men had been too panic-stricken to care about the etiquette of the sea. Some had tried to disguise themselves as women. Some had jumped into the water and been pulled aboard. And there were the sailors who had had to get the boats away. But for the most part, true gentlemen had stayed behind: Jack Phillips the wireless operator, for instance, tapping away at his Morse key over and over and over again: "Come at once. We have struck an iceberg. It's CQD, old man. Position 41° 40'N, 50° 14'W. Come at once. We have struck –" Gentlemen.

Like the ones in the water who had found the rafts too crowded to take another soul, and swum away again, with a cry of "Good luck – God bless you!" Gentlemen.

Like the engineers still labouring to provide power, so that all the lights in the ship could blaze during the evacuation, be seen by rescue ships, raise the spirits of those caught up in the death of the *Titanic*. True gentlemen.

Like the musicians playing even now a jaunty little tune, while the deck beneath them tilted more and more steeply. True gentlemen.

There were wives, too, who chose to stay behind with their husbands.

And men like Ben and Victor, who seeing how some must live and some must die, had thrown off their life-jackets and turned away from the lifeboats. "Tell my wife I played the game out straight to the end," Ben had called to those in the boat. "No women shall be left aboard this ship because Ben Guggenheim is a coward."

The band struck up "Abide with me." The lights were flickering now in some of the portholes. It was two in the morning of 15 April, and the ship was going down. The entire front half disappeared. The stern section stood on end, then, like a still photograph, hesitated for a full five minutes before slipping out of sight.

Built to carry 2,435 passengers and crew, the *Titanic* was equipped with enough life-boats to save just 1,178 people. Of the 2,200 souls who left Southampton on 10 April 1912, bound for New York, only 705 lived. The distress signal was picked up. Help did come, but not until the *Titanic* was 4 kilometres down on the bottom of the Atlantic. The disaster gave rise to new safety regulations, but never again has a ship claimed to be "unsinkable". The *Titanic* had restored people's humility in the face of the pitiless sea.

CQD – "Come Quick, Danger" – were the Morse letters used before the introduction of SOS as the international distress signal.

"Just Going Outside"
1912

There was nothing to be gained by such a journey, except honour and adventure. And yet honour is everything to such men. They wished for the honour of being first to set foot at the South Pole.

So the worst thing that could happen to them, it seemed at the outset, was that the Norwegians would get there first. The competition was so fierce between Captain Scott's team and Roald Amundsen's that the desperate cold, the grit-sharp flying snow, the blinding brightness of the polar plains did not seem the real enemies at all. Scott and Wilson, Evans, Bowers and Oates left their last depot with nine days' supplies, expecting that two long marches would make them the first men in history to visit the South Pole. The excitement lent them an energy they could never otherwise have mustered.

Then they saw it – a black speck in the distance, something which did not belong in the white, untrodden snow of virgin territory. When they got closer, their worst fears were confirmed: it was a flag. There were sledge tracks, too, and paw prints. The desolate Antarctic, last unconquered territory on the planet, was no longer theirs, no longer the prize they had expected after months of agonizing effort. Amundsen was ahead of them.

In a way, it would have been less terrible to turn back then and there, not to have to march on, dragging the cripplingly heavy sledge, eating up more of their dwindling provisions. Then they would not have had to stand at the South Pole and taste the bitterness of defeat. Their achievement was immense, and yet they accounted it "a horrible day" that 17 January when they stood at the bottom of the world amid the footprints of another expedition. The Norwegians had beaten them by just thirty-five days. "All the daydreams must go," wrote Scott in his diary, "it will be a wearisome return."

And so it was. The calm weather which had made it possible to trek so far from help or shelter began to break up. A change of wind blew snow through the fabric of their clothes and filled up their mittens. The weather was deteriorating unexpectedly early, the temperature dropping unimaginably low, the wind stiffening. The cold was unspeakable – unspeakable chiefly because these men were English officers and gentlemen; to have complained or inconvenienced their friends would have been dishonourable. And honour was everything.

Then Edgar Evans died.

Laurence Oates got frostbite in his foot. It had been troubling him even at the Pole; ten weeks later, he could go no further. He knew that he too was going to die, but took comfort from the thought that his regiment might be proud of him. On the night of 6 March, he bedded down, fervently hoping to die in his sleep. Once again luck was against him. He woke to the knowledge that his failure to die promptly would delay his friends – perhaps even prevent them reaching safety themselves. As undemonstrative as ever, he crawled out of his sleeping-bag and got painfully to his feet. A blizzard was blaring outside: a white madness.

"I am just going outside and may be some time," he said.

The others sat up. "No!"

"We can still make it, old boy!"

"You said yourself . . ."

But the tent flap dropped back into place, and Oates was gone: no grand scene, no heroic declamation – "just going outside".

"We knew that poor Oates was walking to his death," wrote Scott, ". . . it was the act of a brave man and an English gentleman."

His self-sacrifice would be wasted if the others did not push on, try to reach the depot. Twenty miles to go. But they knew inwardly, beneath their endlessly cheerful banter, that they would probably not make it. They were down to their last primus-filling of oil and next to no food: a smear of cocoa and lump of pemmican. Scott succumbed to frostbite, but there was such a short way left to go – only fifteen and a half miles! He knew he would lose his foot, but would he lose his life too? Eleven miles.

Wilson and Bowers were planning to go ahead to the depot, for more fuel. But the blizzard shut down, as if the flapping tent of frozen sky had fallen on them. Discussing how they should best finish their doomed expedition, they resolved to go out and meet death face-to-face, to walk, with or without baggage, until they dropped in their tracks. But the blizzard thwarted them. The blizzard had picked up the outside world and shaken it out of existence. Besides, a tent and sledge might be found, whereas three men, falling separately, along an unmarked path would soon be obliterated by the snow, never to be found. So they settled themselves as comfortably as they could and waited. It would not be a long wait.

On 20 March, they had enough tea for two more cups, enough food for two meagre days. On the twenty-ninth the blizzard was still raging, and Scott wrote the last words in his diary: "For God's sake, look after our people."

The snow did all it could to bury the tent, but its flue and a bamboo upright on the sledge still showed above the drifts when a search party found Scott's last camp, eight months later. The three had come to within eleven – about sixteen kilometres – miles of safety.

They lay in their sleeping-bags, letters and diaries intact. Even the worst luck, the worst weather, the worst wilderness in the world could not succeed in erasing the indelible mark left by such courageous men.

As well as his diary, Robert Falcon Scott left a number of letters. "We are pegging out in a very comfortless spot," he wrote to his best friend, J. M. Barrie, author of *Peter Pan* and godfather of his son. "We are showing that Englishmen can still die with a bold spirit, fighting it out to the end."

Great as Amundsen's achievement was, the sheer tragedy of Scott's trip, the cheery, stiff-upper-lip composure of that diary inspired more awe than any success story. Everyone wanted to think that they too, could go out to face death like Oates.

Votes for Women!

1913

Aboard the train there was a holiday atmosphere. Everyone was travelling to the same destination: Epsom Downs. It was Derby Day, and people who never thought of going to the horse-races flocked to Epsom for the grandest race of the year. Families with picnic baskets and six sticky children, clerks and factory workers, young couples smiling shyly at each other, brash men in loud sports coats. No one paid much attention to the young woman sitting in a corner of the carriage, her handkerchief held to her mouth.

"Now, George, I don't want you gambling your money away."

"Just a flutter, dear. Just a flutter."

"Perhaps just a shilling on the King's horse. It's only patriotic to bet on His Majesty's horse . . ."

The young woman's teeth tore a small hole in the corner of her hand-kerchief. Emily Davison stepped down from the

train, and the cheerful crowd swept her along. The green of Epsom Downs was submerged beneath the colourful holiday clothes of the race-goers. The amplified voices of stewards speaking through megaphones sounded like dogs barking. Bookmakers stood on boxes shouting the betting odds they were offering. Bookies' runners gesticulated like lunatics, using their secret sign language. Emily too, had a secret. Someone had daubed "Votes for Women" on the fence. Her fingers brushed the words as the crowd carried her along.

She did not place any bets. She did not sip tea at the cafeteria or look over the horses in the saddling enclosure for a likely winner. Not until the big event – the Derby Sweepstake itself – was about to begin did she worm her way through the crowds to a place by the white rails of the race course. From there she would have a perfect view of the runners thundering down the straight. The crowd gave a single excited cry of "They're off!" and the 1913 Derby had begun.

The King's horse did not take the lead. It was halfway down the field as the runners entered the straight. The crowd to either side of Emily leaned forwards, shouting for the horse they had backed. Perhaps they thought Emily was doing the same.

"Votes for Women!" Her voice came out small and piping. How fast they moved. She had not realized how fast a galloping horse moved. Slipping under the rail, she felt the ground tremble under her feet.

Someone made a grab to pull her back, but she ducked forwards – a small, pale figure in hat and gloves, purse hanging from her wrist. The front-runners tried to avoid her, but the ones behind had no time. She flung herself under the hooves of the King's horse – it was done in a flash – and many in the crowd saw the muddle of hooves and clothes and thought a jockey had come unseated. Then a strange, delayed gasp of revulsion went up, half drowned by the shouts of the spectators down by the winning post, still cheering their horses on.

". . . sheer suicide . . ."

". . . madwoman!"

". . . what possessed her . . ."

". . . anything to draw attention to themselves . . . Is she dead?"

". . . these suffragettes."

The voices reached Emily as if down the dark shaft of a well. The stewards and first-aiders who came to her side were sharp-voiced with disgust. She had spoiled the day for so many people.

Before Emily Wilding Davison died, she was a leading militant in the Women's Social and Political Union founded by Emmeline Pankhurst. Though the campaigners had resorted to arson, slashing paintings, smashing windows, invading Parliament, even street fighting with the police, neither these efforts nor public outrage at the ill-treatment of suffragettes brought about a change. With the outbreak of the First World War, the WSPU ceased its campaigns to help with the war effort. Women made themselves so indispensable while the men were away fighting that afterwards society acknowledged there was no going back. In 1918, women over thirty who were married, householders or university graduates were given the vote. Not until 1928 did all women over twenty-one obtain the vote.

No Man's Land
1914

It was Christmas Day, but nothing to show for it being Christmas. There was no snow, no laughter, no celebration. Nothing to celebrate. The guns had fallen silent, but before long they would be pounding again, shaking the mortar out of the sky, shaking the rats out of their holes, making the dead tremble out on no-man's-land. Rags of torn clothing hung on the barbed wire out there, like bunting, but they hung there every day, gradually losing their colour. It was not Christmas which had put the bunting there. It was the war.

"It will be all over by Christmas," they had said at the beginning. But they had not said *which* Christmas or whether, when it finally ended, there would be anyone left alive to see it.

> *"Stille Nacht, heilige Nacht*
> *Alles schlaft, einsam wacht . . ."*

The soldiers sitting slumped in their swampy trenches, remembering past Christmases, thought at first that the carol was in their imaginations. Then they realized that the singing was real, that it was drifting over from the German trenches on the other side of no-man's-land. The enemy were remembering Christmas, too.

Of course they were. Christmas is universal. And what were they – those German infantrymen over there – but young men far from home, wishing they were somewhere else this vile, wartime Christmas Day in France. Only weeks before, the British Tommies might have believed all that propaganda about Germans murdering babies and burning churches. But they knew better now. The enemy they knew as "Jerry" was just as frightened, just as homesick. He, too, had a wife back somewhere – children maybe – sitting through Christmas Day clutching his mud-spattered letters home and remembering . . .

"Silent night, holy night
All is calm, all is bright . . ."

The Welsh Fusiliers over in the next trench were joining in now. Forever singing, those Taffies. Some of them were singing in Welsh, others in English. Same carol, just different words. Same meaning. Same Christmas.

Suddenly *everyone* burst out singing.

Then a German called out: something about schnapps: something about sharing a drink. He rose up

into view, and the singing petered to a halt. Would he be shot down by a sniper? What sniper? How can you shoot a man when you've just been singing along with him? Other heads rose above the muddy parapets, dirty, fatigued faces looking at one another across the grassless, treeless, lifeless no-man's-land which separated the German trenches from the English ones.

Something round and brown dropped out of the slab-grey sky, and all the heads ducked. Hands flew up to shield vulnerable eyes and ears. Was it a shell? A mortar? The brown globe bounced two or three times, then rolled to a standstill. It was a football.

A football in no-man's-land? Was it English or Welsh or German? It was neutral. No-man's-land is neutral. It belongs to nobody, except perhaps the dead who die out there, hanging on the barbed wire.

First one, then five, then a dozen men scrambled out of their trenches, each one exhorting the men behind to follow. A few hung back – suspicious of an ambush. But enough jogged out on to the barren wasteland, greatcoats dangling stiffly down to their ankles, cigarette smoke curling from the cupped palms of their hands. Enough for a game of football.

Jerry and Tommy exchanged cigarettes, swigs of liquor. Someone marked out goal-mouths with bundled up coats. There were shouts and cheers, and little puffs of smoky breath as the players panted in the cold air. For half an hour or more that game lasted.

Then somewhere far off – far up the line – artillery started up: a gentle *whoomp, whoomp*, like a heartbeat. The smokers dragged deep on their cigarettes and threw them down. The players shook hands, gathered up their greatcoats, pointed to the faint red glare in the distant sky. The sound of gunfire came closer.

Without anyone giving a direct command, the men returned to their respective trenches. They did not hurry. Machine-gunners checked their ammunition. Riflemen eased the springs of their carbines. The Welsh were the last to stop singing.

Nothing had changed. The end of the war had come no closer. There would be no spontaneous laying down of arms in defiance of the commanding officers, no mutinous refusal to fight any more. But something had happened, out there in no-man's-land; something every man there would remember until he died – whether he died next morning out on the wire or lived to see other, peacetime Christmas Days.

The mortars began to thud, crazing the slab-grey sky, making the muddy earth trickle in slurries down into the trenches. Cowering soldiers hunched their shoulders against it and buttoned up their greatcoats. Out on no-man's-land the football lay forgotten, like a Christmas hazelnut after a splendid meal.

The sculptor-artist Henri Gaudier-Brzeska, as well as several other eye-witnesses, wrote of the Christmas Day football match in his letters home. He was killed, aged twenty-four, in 1915, fighting in a war which, between 1914 and 1918, would see nine million die.

Derailing the Country
1926

Time was, it was every boy's dream to drive a railway engine, and one engine in particular: the *Flying Scotsman*. Bob Sheddon, however, saw it as his patriotic duty – to keep the railways running. The strikers had vowed to bring the country to a standstill, but Bob was determined to drive the *Flying Scotsman* from Edinburgh to London on Monday, 10 May.

The view from her twelve carriages that day was of quiet streets, smokeless factory chimneys, silent stockyards. It was like Sunday in the mid-week. The country was holding its breath, waiting to see whether the Government or the trade unions would be the first to back down in their argument over the miners' dispute.

Bob's volunteer fireman was a student from Edinburgh University, Robert Aitken. Some of his friends were working at the docks or driving lorries, helping to defeat the strike. Not that his friends would ever do that kind of work once they had their degrees. Indeed, they might never dirty their hands again with machine oil or crates of fish, but it was a lark – or else their patriotic duty: every volunteer had his own motives for trying to break the General Strike. Some thought the striking miners and transport workers and dockers and factory hands were bloody-minded

Communists trying to bring down the Government and sow the seeds of anarchy. Some thought that the suffering caused to ordinary people – if London, say, ran out of food – was simply not justified. For some it was just a game: to break the strike.

The *Flying Scotsman* rattled along, trailing steam-clouds of glory. "What speed did you say she could do?" said Robert.

"Sixty mile an hour," said Bob. "Not through Dam Dyke, naturally."

The huge, sleek engine sighed steam as she slowed to a mere six miles an hour for the level crossing near Cramlington. That was when they saw it – a gap in the rails ahead.

Robert hung half out of the cab, peering through the steam. "Piece of rail – gone!" he gasped. "We'll never stop in time!"

Bob slammed on the brakes. The gigantic metal

wheels spun on the tracks, and sparks flew. But a steam engine needs time to slow down and stop, even from six mph. She trundled on, wheels skidding, the carriages jolted by the sharp braking. On and on she rolled, until in ponderous slow motion one wheel found no rail under it, and she slumped over sideways. The *Flying Scotsman* jumped the tracks and ploughed into a disused signal box at the side of the line. The first carriage jack-knifed. The guard's van was thrown on to its side. All along the length of the train passengers slithered to the floor. There was a smell of burning and cries of "Fire!"

Police and firemen and ambulances were quick to arrive. So, too, were crowds of onlookers . . . only they did not rush forward to offer help or comfort. They held off at a distance, flapping their caps and grinning. As passengers staggered away, dishevelled and shaken, some in tears, some dazed and expressionless, the crowd began to jeer and whistle. Strikers from nearby Cramlington. Perhaps they were only jeering the driver and volunteer fireman. Or perhaps they deemed the passengers strike-breakers, too, for trying to travel despite the strike.

Sabotage, the police said, carrying away two iron bars and a sledge hammer from near the scene of the crash. Still, no serious harm was done. Only one person was injured. The boilers of the *Flying Scotsman* were doused and she was not much damaged. Copies of the *British Gazette* blew about on the lines and were turned back to pulp by the rain. Tomorrow's edition would say how the *Flying Scotsman* had been derailed by strikers. But there would be other train crashes to report as well. That same Monday, at Bishop's Stortford, a goods train ran into a passenger train and one man was killed. Between Berwick and Edinburgh three people died in a collision.

Were they casualties of the strike or of the strike breakers? It depends on your point of view. Either way, they were just as dead.

The General Strike of 1926 lasted from one minute to midnight on 3 May until twenty past noon on 12 May. A million miners had been told their pay was to be cut to save money. When they refused to accept the pay-cut, they were locked out. Nearly two million workers downed tools in support of them, but the Conservative Government under Prime Minister, Stanley Baldwin, instead of negotiating, set out to break the General Strike. The *British Gazette*, published by the Government, was full of anti-strike propaganda. The Trade Unions published a rival publication: the *British Worker* full of pro-strike propaganda. After nine days of chaos, which split public opinion right down the middle, the General Strike caved in. The miners stayed on strike all summer but in the end poverty defeated them.

Memories of a Jarrow Marcher

1936

When the big cranes came down, I finally grasped the truth. The shipyard was gone, closed, finished, and every man who worked there was out of work for good. Including me.

Grandpa refused to believe it. He kept going down there, oiling things, keeping things serviceable for when it opened up again. Me, I knew better. I was out grubbing up coal dust for fuel. It was risky: I could have been caught and fined, but I couldn't have Mam and the bairns shivering. The lad next door stayed in bed a lot – just to keep warm. You can't feel hungry if you're asleep.

The streets were always ringing empty. Me, I went walking. All the way to Newcastle and back was nothing. We were always good walkers, we Jarrow lads, and it passed the time.

We couldn't move away to seek work. Dad had spent his savings buying the house, but he couldn't have sold it for a ten-shilling note. Who'd want to live in Jarrow where three men in four were out of work?

Mothers didn't eat; they gave what food there was to their menfolk and bairns. This is the twentieth century I'm talking about, and women and babies were so weak with hunger that they died of the least little thing. My sisters Jean and Annie got out. They went south and got work in London as waitresses. Some days, I thought I'd never see them again.

A year went by and nobody at Westminster even troubled to come and see what the shipyard closure had done to us.

Then up gets Joe Symonds – I'll never forget it. "I am prepared to march 7,000 men to London and demand justice!" says Joe. "The working-class people of this town must rise in strength and demand that something be done!"

Well, everyone liked the idea; we all wanted to go. There *could* have been 7,000. But the organizers said thousands would be hard to feed and shelter, so they settled on 200. We drew lots in our house. I won. But our Jack gave me his waterproof, Dad gave me his suit, our Tom gave me his cap. Mam gave me a kiss. So in a way we all went on the Jarrow Crusade.

Red Ellen led us – our MP, Ellen Wilkinson. They called her Red Ellen because of her hair, not because she were a Communist. This had nothing to do with politics, see? This was about starvation. We didn't want charity; we wanted work. We wanted people down south to know what we were suffering up in Jarrow. So we would walk all the way to London and present a petition to Parliament, and along the way we could tell people how we came to be in such a plight.

It put heart into us, just to be *doing* something for a change. We were going to call it the Jarrow Hunger March, but then one of the marshals said "Crusade" would be nicer. So Jarrow Crusade it was. We carried a banner with those two words, ahead of 200 men all in their Sunday best, and the Mayor of Jarrow and Red Ellen – not forgetting Paddy the dog, of course. He was our mascot. He trotted along with us, chipper as you like, all those miles to London.

We walked for fifty minutes, rested for ten, and kept going ten hours a day. Every town we reached, we rushed to the post office to collect letters from our families. That helped with the homesickness. After a while we were all best-muckers – friends to the end! We looked out for each other. Tynesiders might be rough, tough men, but they can be tender as lassies when there's a need.

Jarrow, Chester le Street, Darlington, Ripon, Harrogate, Leeds, Wakefield, Sheffield, Chesterfield, Nottingham . . . Everywhere we stopped, people welcomed us. That "Crusade" idea caught their imagination. Also, we didn't make political speeches. We just told how it was: how many were out of work, how many babies died before their first birthday. People who, up till then, had been calling us a bunch of bolshevik trouble-makers, found themselves cheering Miss Ellen and writing letters to the papers saying, "Something must be done!"

Leicester, Northampton, Bedford, St Albans . . . And folk were so *good* to us! They laid on hot dinners, campsites, sandwiches. A cinema manager let us in free to see a moving picture. A theatre owner sent the artistes round by taxi to give us a show. The Leicester Co-op workers stopped up all night mending our boots. Medical students turned out all along the way to cure our ills, and never charged a penny piece. And we got fit and we got fed and we were treated decent – which is more than we had been back home. We missed our wives and bairns, of course we did, and the walking was hard on the feet, but it was a fine time – a grand time.

Then we reached London.

The police were suspicious of us, but they couldn't stand in our way. We weren't the Peasants' Revolt. We were a bunch of men all spruced up, carrying a message from 11,572 people to their elected government. And any Englishman has a perfect right to petition his government about an injustice.

We had a rally in Hyde Park. That was the best day for me: holiday crowds and music. Someone called my name – and there was Jean and Annie! – along with hundreds of other Jarrow-born lassies and lads who'd gone after the work in London. A few tears flowed, I can tell you!

Then there was that meeting in Farringdon. That put the cap on things. Maybe Sir John thought he was helping; maybe he fancied the cheers. But up stands Sir John Jarvis, MP, and says he's opening a new tube works at Jarrow. The journalists grabbed the news and ran.

Next day the papers were full of it: "Jarrow To Have New Works", it said. So that was all right, wasn't it? The happy ending everyone wanted. The great British public breathed a sigh of relief – and put us clean out of mind.

Next day we were offered a jolly trip on the Thames. We didn't know it was a trick to get us out of the way. When we got back, the petition was already handed in. The politicians had said, "Yes, but look: the Navy will be ordering new ships soon, from some place or other, and Sir John is opening these tube works . . . What more is there to say?"

Billy Thompson – our Mayor – was grand. He showed them his chain-of-office – a chain of little gold hawsers and anchors to represent the thousand ships built in Jarrow. "If you're not going to help us, this means nothing," he said, and dropped it – *clunk* – on the table. Grand gesture. Then we all shuffled off.

Do I sound ungrateful to the great Sir John Jarvis, MP? Well, Sir John's tube works, if they ever opened, would employ 150 men: 150 out of 7,000. And just by talking about it, he had lost us everything. So we took out the ten-shilling notes we had saved for the train

fare, smoothed them flat, and bought our tickets home.

Of course, when the orders for new Navy ships came along, they did not go to Jarrow. Palmer's shipyard had been sold off, hadn't it? All its machinery sold for scrap to the Belgians. The Belgians put in a bid and got the work. Well, they had the machinery, didn't they?

It did no good at all, the Jarrow Crusade. It was a grand effort – got the whole country stirred up – but it did no good. When we got home, the cranes were still gone. The streets of Jarrow were always ringing empty. It was a ghost town. A dead town. Red Ellen said it had been murdered.

Palmer's shipyard was a busy working enterprise. When it ran a little into debt, the bank foreclosed. In October 1936, 207 unemployed men (plus Paddy the mascot) left Jarrow carrying a petition. It represented 7,000 men on the dole in Jarrow, 35,000 hungry mouths. On the way south 90,000 sympathizers signed their names in support of the Crusade. It took a month to reach London. Then the Prime Minister sent it away saying the problem had already been solved.

The Brave Little Boats of Dunkirk

1940

We knew things were going badly when the command came to retreat. Tanks were breaking through our lines, we were passing whole convoys of lorries on fire, and there was shellfire all around. We knew things had gone wrong altogether when they told us to destroy all our kit. But I could barely believe it when I realized that the whole British Expeditionary Force was on the retreat across France.

Each man was supposed to keep one blanket and a full pack: everything else had to be destroyed to keep it out of German hands. Wireless sets lay about with their valves smashed and their insides hanging out. Gunsights had to be broken and the breeches of the big guns blocked with concrete or rocks. I remember Harry and I had nicked a case of wine along the way. We had to smash even that. It drained away into the ground like blood. All the time, droves of miserable, muddy men were streaming by on foot.

The Germans had us pretty much surrounded on three sides. Then it rained again. It rained hard.

Trouble was, the vehicles abandoned by one platoon blocked the roads for the rest of us trying to get west to the coast. It was chaos – mud and confusion. Finally, about twenty-five miles from Dunkirk, the road ahead was clogged solid and we had to pick our way on foot, single-file. Down every road came these single-file streams of men, all converging on Dunkirk like rivers giving into the sea. The beaches, when we got there, were a mass of men. I never saw a crowd like it. My stomach turned to water at the sight. We were sitting ducks! The German army was closing in on us and the German air force could fly over to bomb and machine-gun us whenever they liked. Soon we would all either be dead or taken prisoner. I remember saying to Harry, "This is the end of the war for us, mate."

There were a handful of destroyers off shore, sent to take off as many as possible of us. But there were just so many to be taken off! Already the destroyers were being dive-bombed and sunk.

Harry and I took shelter in the cellar of a house near the beach, waiting for our turn to go aboard the rescue ships. How can I describe it? It was the biggest queue in the world: men waiting to go home, to stay alive. The queue moved forward twenty metres each hour. But it was quite well organized. Food was being shared out and there were pickets on duty to make sure no one jumped the queue.

Oddly, the Germans did not come when we expected. Our air force had lots of planes in the air, trying to protect us from the bombing and machine-gunning. Harry and I broke into a shop and took some deckchairs and food and drink; then we sat and got rather woozy, I have to admit, trying not to think about our chances. Surely, Hitler had won. It's not a wide stretch of water, the English Channel, but it's quite wide

enough. You can't walk home across it. So what escape did we have, realistically?

I was out there three days. Others were there eight or nine. We were like mice trapped in the corner of a room, just waiting for the cat's paw to drop. Still the Germans did not arrive. It was uncanny, inexplicable. Harry said, "Maybe they don't like sand in their boots." Day and night, day and night. The beaches stank of death, noxious smoke, sewage, blood, iodine and wet wool.

Then, do you know what? Other boats started to appear off-shore – not naval ships but private boats – ferries, yachts, tugs, barges, launches. It was like a regatta! Practically every English

boat capable of crossing the Channel
seemed to have come to help pick
up men! All day they kept coming.
All day and all night.

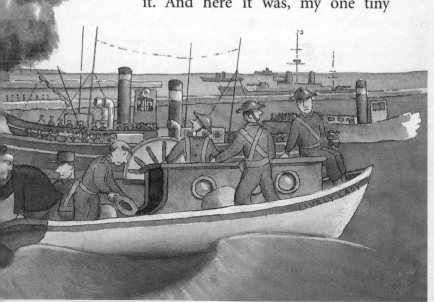

Soldiers were wading out into the water to climb
aboard: some, more organized, were waiting their turn
at the harbour. They waited for the signal, then ran zig-
zagging at full tilt along the harbour wall to some grey
navy ship or millionaire's sleek motor yacht.

When that low-flying bomber came over, the
vibration of its engine made my teeth chatter. It
dropped a bomb ten metres away and I was drenched
in sand. Harry was killed outright. That's when my
nerve broke. I ran into the water,
heading out for a motor-boat put-
putting towards the beach.

It was the kind of boat you
might take for a trip round the
bay. A big sea would have swamped
it. And here it was, my one tiny

chance to get away. Up to my waist. Up to my shoulders. Trying to keep my feet. The water was cold: it climbed inside my clothes, layer by heavy layer. A helmet floated past. I think I trod on a man's kitbag.

There was an old man aboard the motor-boat. He left the helm and came to pull me aboard – me and six or seven others. We were so eager to climb in, and so clumsy, that we nearly overturned him. As he leaned towards me, his face was grey and drawn with fright, cold, uncertainty. I suppose mine was much the same, though, and I was less than half his age.

The beach was a seething mass of men and noise: shouting, explosions. But out on the water, I don't believe we spoke one word all the while the boat was picking its way through the other craft and out to sea. Then the Frenchman beside me started repeating over and over and over again: "*Merci. Merci, merci, merci.*"

Sometimes the old man acknowledged another boat-owner with a nod or a brief wave: sailing people all know each other. There were bankers and factory hands and doctors and teachers and fishermen, sea scouts and taxi-drivers; boys too young for the army and old men who had fought in the last war. There were fireboats and fishing smacks and lifeboats. A lovely old paddle-steamer chugged and splattered past us, like something from an older, sweeter world. Some vessels had been across the Channel several times already, and picked up soldiers and taken them home, then come back for more. The risks were horrific, what with German planes overhead and the shelling. I saw a pleasure boat blown out of the water, a yacht turned over. I saw a destroyer burning on the horizon under a pall of smoke. This was no trip around the bay. I cowered down in the bottom of the boat, my head up against a slopping petrol can. It's not a wide stretch of water, the Channel, but it's wide enough to die in.

The old man told us how he had been listening to the wireless when the call had gone out: "The Admiralty has made an order to all owners of pleasure crafts, fishing boats, or freighters between thirty and one hundred feet in length to report to the Admiralty at Dover."

This was his fourth trip.

I never saw a sight so stirring as the white cliffs of Dover parting the sky from the sea, and the winking of the harbour lights. There was hot food waiting, and first-aid for the wounded as well as blankets and smiles. As I climbed the steps up the harbour wall, I realized that I did not even know the name of the man who had rescued me. I turned to ask, but he was already pushing off again, putting out to sea, heading for the Dunkirk beaches to snatch up a few more lives.

That was four years ago – May 1940. Now I'm going back, too. It is 6 June, and we are all set for the big one – the Allied Invasion of Europe. Back then, the papers called it the miracle of Dunkirk a victory! That was no victory. As Winston Churchill said, "You don't win wars by evacuations." No, Dunkirk was a hellish, humiliating defeat for us. Now the same men are going back over there to take Europe from the Nazis. You want to see what victory looks like? Watch us.

At this point in the Second World War, the advancing Germans were pushing back the British Expeditionary Force thirty to forty miles a day. When Prime Minister Winston Churchill realized he would have to evacuate the troops off Dunkirk beach, he expected to be able to rescue about 45,000 men before the Germans arrived and captured or killed the rest.

To the utter disgust of his generals, Hitler ordered his troops to halt their advance. To this day, no one knows why. Instead of two days, Operation Dynamo (as the evacuation was called) went on for nine tireless days and brought out 338,226 British soldiers. Eventually the Germans did arrive: 45,000 men were captured. But enough had got away to make a real difference to the course of the war. It is just possible that his strategic blunder at Dunkirk lost Hitler the Second World War.

Operation Dynamo cost its heroes dear; approximately 2,000 civilians and British Navy men were killed fetching troops off the beaches; 235 of the 600 brave little boats which set sail were sunk by enemy fire.

Improving on History
(50,000 bc, 1907, 1953)

An expectant hush fell over the lecture hall as Charles Dawson rose to speak. The newspapers had hinted at what he would say, and no one in the world of archaeology wanted to miss it. He peered down at them from the lectern – a man known for his painstaking archaeology, for his thoroughness and attention to detail. He spoke of a gentle afternoon walk in the Sussex countryside. Not the stuff of headlines, surely?

"Two workmen were digging gravel . . . I asked if they had found bones or other fossils there . . . urged them to preserve anything they might find . . .One of the men handed to me a small portion of an unusually thick human parietal bone . . . Some years later, in the autumn of 1911, I picked up another and larger piece . . ."

Science called the find "Dawson's Dawn Man" of Piltdown – *Eoanthropus dawsoni* – a creature neither ape nor man but part-way between the two. Here was the living proof (fossilized proof, anyway) which archaeology had been longing for. Darwin's theory of evolution had been proved, and by a find in the English Sussex countryside!

Nearly one hundred years before, Charles Darwin had put forward the theory that mankind did not spring into existence perfectly formed, out of clay, by the finger of God, but had developed over millions of years, by random accident, from ape into man. Darwin had stirred up a hornet's nest; there were many people, even in 1912, who rejected Darwinianism as a wicked heresy against God. But now Dawson had found the *proof* – an example of a Dawn Man, part ape, part man. Piltdown Man was the missing link in a chain of conclusive evidence: mankind truly was descended from the apes.

The top of the Piltdown skull was shaped like early man's, the jaw like that of an ape. Immediately opinion was split between those who said jaw and skull had washed by chance into the same gravel bed, and those who accepted that jaw and skull belonged together. For a couple of years the controversy raged . . . until Dawson produced a *second* Piltdown skull, and there was no further talk of him having made a mistake. In fact he was the hero of the hour. He had found the missing link!

But shortly, the cataclysm of the First World War pushed Dawson's discovery out of everyone's mind. What did it matter how mankind had originated: the question was, did mankind have a future?

Charles Dawson, briefly feted and famous, fell ill in 1915 and by the following year himself lay buried in the English countryside. Now it was up to his friend and colleague, Arthur Smith Woodward, to defend Piltdown Man from doubting Thomases, to field the questions of palaeontologists wanting to research further. His life's work, whether he chose it or not, became Piltdown Man.

Time passed. In China, Java and Africa other ape-men were found: Darwin's theories were proved time and again. Oddly, though, these new finds had jaws like early man and crania like apes. Well, perhaps primates had evolved by two *different* routes into modern man: one jaw-first, one cranium-first.

Then carbon-dating – a method of testing bone – was developed which could prove, past doubt, whether Dawson's jaw and cranium were of the same age and therefore parts of the same skull. The test was made. To everyone's astonishment, all the bone proved much *younger* than expected.

Those who had always had their doubts began to mutter "hoax". Science steeled itself to study the two Piltdown skulls for signs of forgery. Once they started looking, the signs were easy to find.

The teeth had been filed down with a metal implement. The bones had been stained artificially to a similar colour. The jaw came from an orang-utan; the cranium was no older than the thirteenth century.

In 1953, the myth of Piltdown Man was exploded as a fake, an invention, a hoax. All those papers, all those debates and learned articles and digs had been for nothing.

But why? Why would anyone embark on such a hoax? To discredit a hated rival? As a student prank which got out of hand? Was it a plot by fundamentalist Christians wishing to discredit the whole theory of evolution? Or did someone want so *much* for the proof to be there that he felt driven to plant it himself? Did someone crave the glory of finding it – want his name associated with the most important find in the history of history? Could he not wait for the proof to surface of its own accord? Was it impatience with the slow unravelling of history?

History knit itself up over millions of years; it only unravels at its own measured pace. It will not be hurried, not for the glory of any one historian or to satisfy the curiosity of those most thirsty to know.

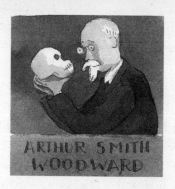

ARTHUR SMITH
WOODWARD

This story illustrates that, even in the twentieth century, there are still those who, for reasons of their own, want to improve on history, falsify the facts to achieve a simple and satisfying perspective on the past.

It has never been firmly proved who perpetrated the Piltdown hoax – one man, two or more – nor why they did it. Dawson is not the only suspect, though Woodward certainly had no part in it. Nowadays, forensic science would have exposed the hoax within weeks, but that does not mean it was the last lie told – not by any means. Manipulating history, tilting it to make a particular argument run true, is as popular as ever. History will always be a prey to liars, storytellers and wishful thinkers.

Breaking the Time Barrier
1954

Roger Bannister sharpened his running spikes on a grindstone in the hospital laboratory. The weather was all wrong for running. This would not be the day when he ran his fastest race. But he went on sharpening his spikes ... just in case the weather changed.

He was a medical student. His final exams were coming up. Soon the gruelling duties of being a young hospital doctor would leave no time for sport. So this might be his last summer's running. It would have been good to prove himself – to perform the impossible.

Bannister sighed and laid the spikes aside. What difference would sharp spikes make, when there was a gale blowing?

At the running track in Oxford, the wind tugged violently at the flag on the church roof. Bannister tried on his new, super-light running shoes, but his mind was pretty much made up: too windy for a record-attempt. At 5.15 p.m. it rained.

Watching the competitors limber up, the crowd was restless, keyed up. They had come there to see Bannister break the record for the mile. This was where he had run his first races as an Oxford student, so they were willing him on. They wanted him to perform the impossible tonight, in Oxford, in front of their very eyes.

If only they understood what they were asking! Only

once would Bannister be able to pour all his nervous energy, his physical strength, his terror into making this run. If he tried and failed, it would not be in him to try again.

The flag on the church was wavering, the wind gusting more gently now. Bannister made his decision. He would try to run the mile in less than four minutes: a feat which had never been done, in the whole history of running.

The runners lined up. Perfect silence. *Bang!* . . . *Bang!* Two pistol cracks. A false start. A surge of fury went through Bannister.

The runners lined up again. This time there was no mistake. His friend Chris Brasher took the lead, setting the pace. "Faster!" hissed Bannister in his ear, but Brasher would not speed up, knowing that if Bannister sprinted too soon, his stamina would not last the mile. "Relax!" called a friend from the crowd.

The Oxford crowd was willing him on. Even the wind held its breath. But Bannister was barely aware of his surroundings. At the half-mile mark he knew he was in with a chance. His legs seemed to be working independently; the ground had no hold on them. His mind was detached. In a kind of trance he took over the lead, put in his final burst of speed.

The winning tape seemed to recede with every step. He must not slow, must not falter. His lungs had to go on feeding his blood; his heart had to go on pumping the oxygen round. This was his one chance in life to do a thing supremely well. If he failed, the world would turn a cold shoulder against him. The winning line taunted him . . .

He snapped the tape with his chest, snapped that invisible barrier everyone had said could not be broken. He had broken the four-minute mile.

It was then he realized – while pain wrung his muscles, and his lungs raged for air – while he collapsed into semi-consciousness – why he had been driving himself for eight years, why he had expended so much effort on achieving this moment. Suddenly he was free of the need to prove anything, free of the need to test himself, free of wanting something so very much. He was utterly, perfectly happy. Even though the crowd saw someone in a state of desperate, agonizing exhaustion, Roger Bannister was happier than he had ever been in his life. The tannoy announced: "Results of the one mile. In first place, Bannister with the time of three minutes . . ." The crowd's cheering drowned out the rest. Split seconds did not matter. For the first time a man had run one mile in less than four minutes.

Roger Bannister was part of a remarkable flowering of English running talent during the 'fifties. The previous year he had failed to win a medal at the Olympic Games – a disappointment made worse by carping public criticism of his go-it-alone attitude. But after the four-minute mile he needed a suitcase to carry all the fan mail. One specially minted, costly trophy had to be given back, because in those days the maximum value of any prize won by an amateur was just £12.

His running mates that night also became household names. Chris Brasher organized the London Marathons, Chris Chataway, another pace setter, became a Cabinet Minister. The 3 minute 59.4 second record was soon broken again, once the psychological four-minute barrier had fallen, but it is Bannister who is remembered best from that era of sporting excellence.

He went on to become a neurologist.

Teaching the World to Sing
1984

It was October. The first Christmas goods were appearing in the shops. Soon everybody would be out there again, spending too much money.

Bob Geldof sat in his London flat watching the television news. It was not Christmassy, the news. Famine and war. In Ethiopia and the Sudan several million people were about to starve to death. On the screen, withered, skeletal babies lay on the ground, fly-blown, grotesque, too weak to cry. Their mothers, old women in their twenties, looked at the camera expressionless; they had long since despaired of anyone helping them. They simply sat and watched their children die.

Viewers everywhere reached for their cheque books, knowing anything they could do would be too little too late: a futile gesture. Geldof reached for the telephone instead. He booked himself a flight to Ethiopia, and went there to see for himself. All the way there, all the way back, all the time he walked among the stench of death, he thought what everyone else was thinking: something ought to be done.

The difference was, Geldof did it.

When he got home, he called up his friends – his famous, glamorous, glitzy, talented, show-business, star-rated friends. He did not ask them for money. He asked them for their time. "There's this number I want to record," he said.

They called the group, "Band Aid". The song was titled, "Do they know it's Christmas?" It was in honour of those people for whom there can be no such thing as a happy Christmas.

It was performed by a larger number of famous recording artists than had ever gathered on one stage before. And the public loved it. It sold more copies than any other recording that year. And every penny of the £10 million profit went to Africa for famine relief.

What is more, it was fun to do! It was like one great party, where everybody arrives in party mood. Even

Geldof had not foreseen how much fun it would be or how much money it would raise. He had to form a trust just to handle the proceeds. Somehow he had tapped into the conscience of the entire Western world.

But the world's poor swallowed it down like one drop of rain falling on a desert. So how could he say Band Aid was over, draw a line under it, call it a day?

Out of Band Aid grew Live Aid. One year later Geldof organized a sixteen-hour concert to be played live and screened all over the world. No one said no to Bob. People gave, free-of-charge, satellite time, studio time, technical support, transport, secretarial services . . . In a matter of weeks the idea took shape: not one, but two concerts – one in Wembley Stadium, London, the other in JFK Stadium, Philadelphia. Phil Collins sat down at a piano and sang in Wembley. Then he got on a plane and flew to Philadelphia, walked on to the stage in the JFK and sang the same song. The watching millions could not believe their eyes.

The truth was, the world had shrunk to such an extent that the people of a hundred nations were sitting together on one couch to watch TV and join in the singing. Forty per cent of the world's population were invited to that party, were asked by their favourite pop idols, heroes and statesmen to give money and to save lives.

It did not just "happen", of course. Celebrities did not simply roll out of bed and decide to go along. For ten weeks, hundreds of technicians, lawyers, politicians, secretaries, singers worked non-stop to make it happen. Not all of them were rock fans. ("I didn't even know who Geldof was," said the American producer of Live

Aid. ("My son did, but I didn't.") But the goodwill was there, because people knew it was going to work. It had the energy of youth behind it. And no one said no to Bob.

Well, perhaps there was one. During the concert, a light aircraft would persist in cruising over the JFK stadium towing advertising banners. The pilot refused to go away. So Bob Geldof asked Ronald Reagan, President of the United States, to telephone the airfield. He did. Within minutes, the light aeroplane was gone.

It was fun to do and it was fun to watch. It was the biggest party the world had ever known. And every pound, dollar and rouble, every shekel, lira and krona of the £48 million raised was going to put food in the mouths of starving children.

"Where do I go and what do I do?" asked superstar Dionne Warwick stepping out of a taxi. Everyone wants to help, if only someone is there to tell them how.

BOB GELDOF

Out of Live Aid and Band Aid came Sport Aid – another £21 million – raised by running ten-kilometre races in nearly 300 cities throughout the world. These were phenomenal fund-raising efforts, galvanizing all the great names of the moment – far too many to list. They did not put an end to world poverty, but they did save thousands of lives. It was possible to invest in communities for the future, as well as saving them from destruction. They also made a whole generation confront the problem of world hunger, its root causes, and how much the developed world can do to ease it.

Set in a Silver Sea
1993

It was as though the *Braer*'s heart failed her in the face
of the storm. Her engines fell silent and left only the
miscellaneous clanking of a big metal ship adrift in a
mountainous sea. For six hours she drifted, while those
aboard and those on shore struggled to stave off
disaster. Could a tug be got out to her? Could a tow line
be attached? Could the engines be restarted?

But every minute, the sea was shouldering the *Braer*
inexorably towards land, shoving and bullying her into
the shallows. With a noise of rending metal, it ran her
aground on the rocks of Garths Ness, stoving in her
watertight sides. She bled black blood.

Oil, in thick clots, haemorrhaged out of her. Every
wave carried some of the *Braer*'s cargo ashore and
daubed it on the rocks, on the weeds, on the sand. Hour
by hour, the *Braer* broke up.

Though the sea was rough, a black ring of calm lay
around the stranded ship like an evil spell. The
coastline, wild, beautiful and little visited till now,
withered. The oil crawled in at the noses of seals and
the gills of fish, larded the sea birds which landed on
the flattened, oily waves, scalded all the fronded sea-
plants, fish eggs and shrimps. Crustaceans let go their
grip on the oily rocks and rattled away like black
pennies on to the sea bed.

Disaster. An ecological tragedy. Those who went to the coast after the stranding of the tanker waded through an oily slick which pulsed with small animals in the last throes of death. They bewailed the devastation – done in a day, but never, surely, to be undone. At best, Garths Ness would take decades to recover: no wildlife, no livelihood for the fishermen, no delight to the senses – just the stench of oil and dead things.

Five years later, an independent survey team went looking for the long-term effects of the *Braer* oil-spill. With more and more oil tankers plying the world's seas, such accidents are bound to happen increasingly often. So it is essential to know what other stretches of cliffs, inlets, bird colonies and fishing communities can look forward to. The worst had to be looked in the face.

The survey found . . . nothing.

Not a trace of oil remained. The sea's surf had scoured clean each pebble and shell. Its tides had dragged the black slime deep into its digestion, and its tide rips had shredded the slick into infinitesimal smallness. Fish shoals had come back. Birds had nested on the cliffs. A profusion of shellfish were busy muscling each other off the shining rocks.

The oil, prehistoric product of a million acres of primaeval forest, had become once again harmless vegetable matter – harmless as dead leaves in autumn crumbling into mulch.

The sea had proved so full of life, that though it had drunk poison, it had failed to die.

The *Braer* oil tanker was stranded at Garths Ness in the Shetlands on 5 January 1993. Science fully expected the oil-spill to do lasting damage, but all the gloomy predictions were proved wrong by the phenomenon of the self-cleansing sea. The story told here does not mean that the sea can digest any amount of pollution. (Every metre of the Atlantic sea lanes between England and America is now polluted, and inshore fishing has been seriously affected.) What it does prove is that nature has powers of regeneration which surpass our wildest imaginings.